We Light the Candles

DEVOTIONS RELATED TO FAMILY USE OF THE ADVENT WREATH

by Catharine Brandt

AUGSBURG FORTRESS, PUBLISHERS
Minneapolis, Minnesota

Scripture quotations are from the Revised Standard Version of the Bible, © 1946, 1952, 1971, and are used by permission.

WE LIGHT THE CANDLES

Devotions related to Family Use
of the Advent Wreath

Freshly cut evergreen boughs . . . brilliant greens and holly studded with red berries . . . their cheerful appearance and pungent odors in homes during the winter excite memories and expectations.

Many families fashion evergreen boughs into an Advent wreath. The circle of boughs is a reminder of God's unending love for us and of the gift of everlasting life he gave us through his Son Jesus Christ.

The word *Advent* means coming—Christ's coming to earth as a baby *for* us, his coming *in* the believer's heart today, and his coming *again* in power and great glory.

Our preparations for Christ's coming can be enriched if we gather around an Advent wreath each day for family devotions. The devotions will focus our attention on our relationship with God. Each candle on the wreath is intended to signify a particular aspect of that relationship.

There seems to be no universal tradition for the color of the candles, or their names. Some use violet candles, some red or white. Some have called the four candles prophecy, Bethlehem, shepherds, angels. Others substitute history, new birth, second coming, faith, peace, joy for one or more candles. Candles more and more have come to symbolize Christ as the Light of the world.

In this booklet the four candles are labeled *promise, light, love,* and *hope.*

This Advent season the family may spend a little time together each day reading Old Testament prophecies and New Testament fulfillments, a little time singing Advent songs, lighting the Advent candles, and talking to God. Some families find the time after breakfast most convenient. Other families choose the moments after dinner. Still others prefer bedtime.

Everyone in the family may have a part in the devotions. One child may light the candles, another snuff them out. A child may read the Scripture passage, offer the prayer, or choose an Advent song. Parents or older children may read the meditation or tell it in their own words.

The length of the Advent season, which begins on the fourth Sunday before Christmas, is determined by the day of Christmas. The daily devotions may be followed through the day before Christmas Eve. Then the one for Christmas Eve may be read.

(Assign one person to light the first candle a little later.)

*READ: Before we light the first candle of Advent, let's listen to the story of a family who received an Advent wreath from their friends.

On the first Sunday in December that year, our doorbell rang. At the door stood a family we knew well—father, mother, and four children—bundled up with caps and mittens.

"Come in. Come in," we cried.

Two of the children carried a bulky package. "We made it for you," they said.

What could it be? Stripping away the wrappings, my husband held up an evergreen wreath attached by red ribbons to a little stand. The fragrance of the wreath filled the room.

"It's an Advent wreath," Jeff said. "You light the candles and talk about Jesus."

"We sawed the boards and pounded the nails," Ben said with a swagger.

"I helped paint the stand red," Connie said.

Little Mary squirmed out of her mother's lap, and shyly held out four candles.

"Our family has never used an Advent wreath," I said. "Tell me all about it so we'll know what to do."

Would our family be able to explain how an Advent wreath is used? *(Members of the family may respond.)*

Now let's light the first candle on our Advent wreath. *(Person who has been chosen to light candle may do so.)* We call the first candle *promise* to remind us that God promised to send his Son Jesus.

* *The introduction has suggestions for family participation.*

6

Long ago the prophet Isaiah spoke these words of promise about Jesus to God's people.

For to us a child is born, to us a son is given; and the government will be upon his shoulder, and his name will be called "Wonderful Counselor, Mighty God, Everlasting Father, Prince of Peace" (Isaiah 9:6).

Long before Jesus was born, God promised it would be so. People joyfully celebrate Christmas because God gave the world his own Son, the very first Christmas gift. We make room for him in our hearts.

SING: Joy to the world! the Lord is come;
    Let earth receive her King;
    Let every heart prepare him room,
    And heaven and nature sing,
    And heaven and nature sing,
    And heaven, and heaven and nature sing.

PRAY: Dear heavenly Father, as we begin the Advent season, teach us the true meaning of Christmas. Each time we light the candle of promise, help us to think about your promise to send Jesus your Son. Amen.

READ: Tomorrow and the rest of the week we'll talk about some other promises God made. We'll light the candle each day to remind us of them.

Each Sunday we'll light one more candle so that the week before Christmas all four candles will be lighted. As we talk about the meaning of the candle, we'll read what God says in the Bible about that meaning. We could keep the Advent wreath here as a centerpiece to remind us of what we learn during Advent.

(The family waits quietly while the candle is put out.)

7

READ *(as someone lights the candle):* We light the candle of
promise to remind us that sometimes people must wait a
long time for God's promises to be kept.

Sing for joy, O heavens, and exult, O earth;
break forth, O mountains, into singing!
For the Lord has comforted his people,
and will have compassion on his afflicted (Isaiah 49:13).

One day in a supermarket a small child howled, and tears
ran down her cheeks. Standing beside a mechanical horse,
she tugged at her mother's coat. "You promised me.
You promised."

"Be still," her mother said. "I don't have any change."

Parents sometimes forget a promise or fail to keep one.
But God is not like that. He keeps his promises.

A long time ago God promised to send his people a Savior
who would set them free from sin and death.

God often made his promises directly to people. Other
times he told his prophets what to say. God chose special men
to be his prophets, to give the people his message about things
in the future. Isaiah was one of God's prophets.

Today we can learn about God's promises by reading the
Bible. It tells the story of God's people waiting for him to keep
his promise to send Jesus the Savior. The Israelites did not
know when God would send the Savior, but they waited
expectantly for the promise to be kept.

SING: *First stanza of "O come, O come, Emmanuel,"*
printed on page 38.

PRAY: O God, we know you did keep your promise to send
your Son to save us. Help us to get ready in our hearts
to celebrate his birthday. Amen.

READ (*as someone lights the candle*): We light the first candle of Advent, the candle of promise. This candle reminds us that God used the prophets to tell his promises to the people.

In the Bible we can read some of God's promises about the birth of Jesus the Savior, which the prophets spoke to the people.

"Therefore the Lord himself will give you a sign. Behold, a young woman shall conceive and bear a son, and shall call his name Immanuel." [Immanuel means "God with us."] (Isaiah 7:14).

But you, O Bethlehem Ephrathah, who are little to be among the clans of Judah, from you shall come forth for me one who is to be ruler in Israel, whose origin is from of old, from ancient days. (Micah 5:2).

The words from the Bible which we have just read were promises God told the prophets to give the people. Scribes wrote the promises on parchments, so they wouldn't be forgotten.

The Jewish people read the scribes' parchments and thought and talked about the promises God had given through the prophets. They did not forget that God had promised to send them Jesus the Savior. Their name for the Savior was Emmanuel, which means "God with us."

SING: *Second stanza of "O come, O come, Emmanuel," printed on page 38.*

PRAY: Dear God, thank you for the prophets who told about your promises. Thank you for sending the world the Savior for whom people waited so long. Amen.

READ *(as someone lights the candle):* The candle of promise
reminds us of God's promise to save us from sin.

God has a wonderful plan for our salvation. He chose John
the Baptist before he was born to go before Jesus and prepare
his way. John the Baptist helped people understand
they need forgiveness of sins.

**"You will go before the Lord to prepare his ways, to give
knowledge of salvation to his people in the forgiveness
of their sins"** (Luke 1:76-77).

Zechariah, a priest in the temple, and his wife Elizabeth
were very old. They had no children, though they prayed
for a son.

One day Zechariah was praying in the temple. All at once
the angel Gabriel stood beside the altar.

"Don't be afraid," the angel said. "God has heard your
prayer. Elizabeth will bear a son, and you shall name him
John. He shall prepare the way for the Lord."

When their son was born, Zechariah and Elizabeth named
him John, as the angel Gabriel had told them to do.

John grew up to be John the Baptist, a prophet of the Lord.
He prepared the way for the Lord Jesus, helping people
get ready for Christ's coming by telling them they must stop
doing wrong and must be sorry for their sins. "Repent,"
he cried. "The King is coming, who will take away
the sins of the world."

PRAY: Dear God, you must love us very much to have
planned for our salvation. Thank you for keeping your promise
to save us from sin. Amen.

SING: *Third stanza of "O come, O come, Emmanuel,"
printed on page 38.*

READ (*as someone lights the candle*): This is the candle of promise. God used Mary and Joseph as helpers to carry out his promise to send his Son Jesus.

"You shall call his name Jesus. He will be great and will be called the Son of the Most High; and the Lord God will give to him the throne of his father David" (Luke 1:31-32).

One day God sent the angel Gabriel to Mary, a young woman engaged to Joseph. The shining light about the angel frightened Mary.

"Don't be afraid," the angel said. "God has chosen you to be the mother of his Son."

At first Mary was too surprised to speak. She was to be the mother of Jesus, the long-expected Savior. At last she said, "I am the Lord's servant. I'm ready to do what he wants."

Then God sent an angel to tell Joseph too. "Mary's baby is from God. You shall call him Jesus, for he shall save his people from their sins."

When it was almost time for the baby to be born, Joseph and Mary traveled to Bethlehem to register for taxes. Joseph looked for a place for them to stay, but the innkeeper said, "No vacancy. No room." The only place was a stable back of the inn.

On that special night, there in the stable, God kept his promise. Jesus, God's son, was born.

PRAY: Dear God, thank you for Mary and Joseph who obeyed you. Thank you for keeping your promise and sending us your Son. Amen.

SING: *Fourth stanza of "O come, O come, Emmanuel,"* *printed on page 38.*

READ *(as someone lights the candle):* The first candle of Advent reminds us of how God told the shepherds that he had kept his promise to send Jesus.

"For to you is born this day in the city of David a Savior, who is Christ the Lord" (Luke 2:11).

To a few shepherds who were taking care of their sheep at night on the hills near Bethlehem, an angel announced that God had kept his promise.

All at once the sky blazed like a giant spotlight beaming down on the shepherds. They covered their eyes and shook with fear.

"Don't be afraid," an angel said. "I bring you good news of a great joy for all people." Gradually the shepherds became accustomed to the glorious light, and they looked up. "You will find a babe wrapped in swaddling cloths, lying in a manger."

Then the shepherds saw hundreds of angels in the sky, saying, "Glory to God in the highest and on earth peace." Then the angels left, and the night was dark again.

The shepherds sprang up. "Let's go to Bethlehem and see." Clumping down the hills they hurried toward Bethlehem. When they reached the stable, they stood still. They tugged off their caps, and some of the shepherds knelt. Deep inside they knew that what the angel had told them was true. Here was the Savior, Christ the Lord.

PRAY: Dear God, thank you for giving the good news of Christ's birth to the shepherds and to all of us. Amen.

SING: *"Joy to the world," printed on page 7, or "Hark, the herald angels sing."*

READ *(as someone lights the candle):* We light the first candle
of Advent and remember God's promise to Simeon.

**"Lord, now lettest thou thy servant depart in peace, according
to thy word; for mine eyes have seen thy salvation"** (Luke 2:29-30).

When Jesus was a little over a month old, it was time for
Mary and Joseph to take him to the temple in Jerusalem
to be blessed.

Just as they brought Jesus into the temple, an old man,
a prophet, stopped them. The Holy Spirit had told him to
come to the temple at that very time.

"I am Simeon," he said. "All my life I have looked for the
Savior, the Messiah. God's Holy Spirit has told me I will not
die until I have seen him."

Then gently he took the baby Jesus from Mary's arms and
began to pray. "Lord, now I can die content! For I have seen
with my own eyes the Savior you have given the world!"

Mary and Joseph stood speechless. Even this man in the
temple in Jerusalem knew about their very special son.

Then, guided by the Holy Spirit, Simeon spoke some promises of God. Looking at Jesus, he said, "He is the light that
will shine upon the nations, and he will be the glory of your
special people, called Israel!" Simeon continued to Mary,
"This child shall be hated by many . . . but he will be the
greatest joy to others."

PRAY: O God, give us faith and patience like Simeon, who
waited for your promises to be kept. Amen.

SING: *Stanzas one and four of "O come, O come, Emmanuel,"
printed on page 38.*

READ (*as someone lights the two candles*): Now it is the second week of Advent, so we light two candles on the Advent wreath—the candle of promise and the candle of light. The candle of light reminds us of the star the Wise Men followed.

Wise men from the East came to Jerusalem, saying, "Where is he who has been born king of the Jews? For we have seen his star in the East, and have come to worship him" (Matthew 2:1b-2).

God used a very special kind of light to let the Wise Men know it was time for Jesus the king to be born. They had watched the stars and the skies for a long time. Finally the great and unusual light they were waiting for appeared in the sky. The Wise Men got ready for the long journey over the desert, mounted their camels, and set out.

Naturally they thought Jesus would be in Jerusalem where the temple was, and they went there first. They almost got in trouble with wicked King Herod, who didn't like the idea of a new king of the Jews. But God warned the Wise Men in a dream to stay away from King Herod. They kept their eyes on the bright star that led them to the place where Jesus was.

The Bible doesn't say when the Wise Men came, how many of them there were, or where they came from—only that they visited the little family, that they brought three gifts, and worshiped Jesus.

SING: We three kings of Orient are;
            Bearing gifts we traverse afar,
            Field and fountain,
            Moor and mountain,
            Following yonder star.

               O star of wonder, star of night,
               Star with royal beauty bright,
               Westward leading, still proceeding,
               Guide us to thy perfect light!

(The candle of promise may be lit.)

READ *(as someone lights the second candle):* This is the candle
of light. As we light it, we remember that God sent Jesus
his Son to save all people.

**And nations shall come to your light, and kings to the
brightness of your rising** (Isaiah 60:3).

The Wise Men who followed the light of the star traveled
a long way to find Jesus. They were from a land far away
from the one where Jesus lived. The Bible doesn't say which
country the Wise Men came from, only that it was in the East.

Legends and stories about the Wise Men often say that
each Wise Man was from a different land. In famous paintings
artists have pictured the Wise Men as three kings dressed in
rich robes, wearing crowns, and attended by servants bearing
costly gifts. One king is an Ethiopian, a black man; one is
olive-skinned, an Oriental; and one is white-skinned. In this
way artists tried to show that Jesus came to save all people.

SING: *First stanza of "Thou didst leave thy throne,"
printed on page 39.*

PRAY: Dear God, when the Wise Men saw the light of Jesus'
star, they knew that a great king had been born. Thank you
for sending your Son Jesus to save people everywhere. Amen.

(Appoint one person to light the candles later. Turn off all the lights.)

READ: It's dark, isn't it? It's hard to see without light.
(Now the candles may be lit.)

This is the candle of promise. This is the candle of light. The light of God's love is more powerful than the darkness of sin. The flames of our candles are tiny, but they help us see better. The dark can't chase the light away. The prophet Isaiah talked about people in darkness.

The people who walked in darkness have seen a great light; those who dwelt in a land of deep darkness, on them has light shined (Isaiah 9:2).

The prophet wasn't talking about the dark we have when all the lights are off and the candles aren't lighted.

No, he was talking about the darkness of sin. Long ago people became sinful, and sin darkened their hearts. People were wicked then just as they are today. They hated one another and fought each other in wars. God said they walked in darkness, the darkness of sin.

Jesus came to earth so we could be forgiven for our sins. Because he rescues us from the darkness of sin, we say Jesus is the Light of the world.

SING: *First stanza of "Thou didst leave thy throne," printed on page 39.*

PRAY: Dear God, sometimes we take light for granted. Please remind us how dark our lives would be without the light of love and forgiveness that Jesus brings. Amen.

(The candle of promise may be lit.)

READ *(as someone lights the second candle):* This is the candle of light. A little light comes from it. This candle reminds us that Jesus takes away the fear of darkness and gives us the light of life.

Jesus spoke to them, saying, "I am the light of the world; he who follows me will not walk in darkness, but will have the light of life" (John 8:12b).

In Ethiopia the villages are very dark at night. There are no bright lights, no 100-watt bulbs to screw into electric lamps.

In the bush country when night falls, all movement ends. Men and women and children huddle together in huts or go to sleep. The only light is from the dying coals of the fire on which the evening meal was cooked. Or there may be a tiny flickering light from a little wick in a saucer of oil.

People in the villages are afraid of the dark, because they can't see what's there.

When missionaries talk about Jesus, the Light of the world, that means something to the Ethiopians, because they know how frightening darkness is.

When Jesus guides our lives, he drives out the fear of darkness—darkness around people and darkness inside the heart. Jesus saves us from fear. He gives us the light of life.

SING: *Second stanza of "Thou didst leave thy throne," printed on page 39.*

PRAY: Dear Lord Jesus, be the guiding light of our lives. Help us to love you and serve you so we can always walk in your light.

(The candle of promise may be lit.)

READ *(as someone lights the second candle):* We light the second candle of Advent, the candle of light. We remember that Jesus, the Light of the world, wants us to keep our hearts always open to him.

"Behold, I stand at the door and knock; if any one hears my voice and opens the door, I will come in to him" (Revelation 3:20).

A famous painting hangs in Keble College at Oxford, England. It is called *The Light of the World.*

The artist, William Holman Hunt, has painted Christ wearing kingly robes and a crown of thorns, knocking at a door. The door has no knob, and its hinges are rusty. Weeds overrun the threshold, showing the owner has not opened the door for a long time. Christ is holding a lighted lantern, and light shines around his head. The brightest light, though, shines from his face.

The door represents the door to the human heart. Christ stands outside, but there is no handle on the heart's door. Jesus cannot come in until you ask him. He loves us and wants to be close to us.

If you believe that Christ was born to be your Savior, and that he died for your sins, you can do what the painting suggests. When the heart's door is opened, something wonderful happens. Christ, the Light of the world, will come in.

PRAY: Lord Jesus, help us remember that you are the Light of the world. Help us to keep our hearts always open to you. Amen.

SING: *Second stanza of "Thou didst leave thy throne,"* printed on page 39.

READ *(as someone lights the candles):* Light brings joy. We can be joyful because we know God has saved us from sin.

"For he is Lord of lords, King of kings" (Revelation 17:14).

One Christmas a friend of mine received a card a young girl had made. On the card the little girl had printed: "I wish you did not have to go on the cross. I love you."

Then she had drawn a cross with a man on it. At the bottom of the page she had copied these words: "The God of Christmas joy is also the God of Good Friday sorrow."

What did the card mean?

At Christmas we think of the baby in the manger, and our hearts are filled with joy when we remember how much God loved us. But Jesus wasn't a baby forever. He grew up to be the man Jesus Christ, who came to give his life for us. There wasn't any other way for us to be saved, so Jesus died on the cross for our sins.

We feel a dark sadness because of the painful death Jesus had to suffer. But our hearts are filled with the light of joy when we think of his Easter resurrection. That's why we sing "Hallelujah!" *Hallelujah* means "praise the Lord."

PRAY: Dear God, thank you for the light of joy your gift of salvation brings us. Amen.

SING: *Third stanza of "Thou didst leave thy throne," printed on page 39.*

(The candle of promise may be lit.)

READ *(as someone lights the second candle):* The candle of light reminds us that the light of God's love will show in our lives when Jesus is guiding us.

"Let your light so shine before men, that they may see your good works and give glory to your Father who is in heaven" (Matthew 5:16).

Have you ever watched a prism with the sun shining on it? Prisms cut in fancy shapes are often used to decorate light fixtures or lamps. When the sun shines on a prism, red, blue, green, and purple forms and patterns skip around on the wall.

A diamond or a piece of broken glass will pick up the light's rays and send bright spots bouncing around the room.

The prism, the diamond, or the glass refracts the light. None of these have any light of their own. It's only when a bright light shines through them that people see the reflected lights.

We don't have any light of our own, but when the light of Jesus is in our hearts, we will reflect his light. When Jesus is guiding us, the light of his love shows in our lives.

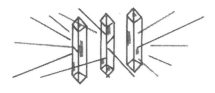

PRAY: This little light of mine, I'm going to let it shine— for Jesus. Amen.

SING: *Third stanza of "Thou didst leave thy throne," printed on page 39.*

(The candle of promise and the candle of light may be lit.)

For God so loved the world that he gave his only Son, that whoever believes in him should not perish but have eternal life (John 3:16).

READ *(as someone lights the third candle):* We call the third candle of Advent, *love.* As the candle of love is lit, let's think about how much God loves each of us.

This week we will be singing the Christmas hymn, "O little town of Bethlehem." The writer of the words, Phillips Brooks, the rector of a church in Philadelphia, visited Palestine. One evening at dusk he rode on horseback past the olive trees outside Bethlehem to the fields where it is believed the shepherds watched their flocks and heard the angel's message.

He thought about the wonderful gift of love God gave to all people that night. He tried to imagine what it had been like in those fields when angels told the shepherds that, because of his love for us, God sent his only Son to save us.

When Phillips Brooks returned to Philadelphia, he often remembered the quiet beauty of that night when he had stood in the shepherds' fields near Bethlehem. He thought of how God's love for all people has continued through the centuries since that first Christmas long ago.

One Christmas season he wrote the words of a song for the children of his church to sing at the Christmas program. He asked the church organist, Lewis H. Redner, to compose the music. The organist had trouble finding a tune he liked. Finally before going to bed he prayed about it. In the night he woke up, a tune in his mind. Quickly he wrote it down. And the children sang the song at the program.

Neither the minister who wrote the words, nor the organist

who composed the music expected anything great from the little song, but people liked it at once. For more than one hundred years it has been a favorite Christmas song.

SING: *First stanza of "O little town of Bethlehem,"* *printed on page 39.*

PRAY: Dear Lord, thank you for Christmas songs that remind us of your great love for us. Amen.

READ *(as someone lights the candle):* We light the candle of promise to remind us of God's wonderful promises.

We light the candle of light to remind us that Jesus is the Light of the world.

We light the candle of love to remind us that God wants us to love him.

We love, because he first loved us (1 John 4:19).

Have you ever tried to walk or swim in the ocean against the tide? Or, have you tried to wade against the current of a fast-flowing stream? The power of the rushing water makes it almost impossible to move in the opposite direction.

God's love for us is very powerful, stronger than any ocean tide or stream current. He doesn't want us to fight against his love or try to ignore it. He wants us to love him too.

In comparison to God's love, our love may seem weak and unimportant. Sometimes we might think God wouldn't care if we didn't love him. But our love is very important to God. He wants us to love him more than anyone or anything else.

PRAY: Dear Lord, in our excitement of getting ready for Christmas, help us not to forget whose birthday we celebrate. We know that you love us, and we want to love you. Help us to show our love for you in our lives.

SING: *Second stanza of "O little town of Bethlehem," printed on page 40.*

(During today's devotion paper and some pencils will be needed. The candle of promise and the candle of light may be lit.)

READ *(as someone lights the third candle):* The candle of love reminds us that God wants us to be kind and loving to our family and friends.

Be kind to one another, tenderhearted, forgiving one another as God in Christ forgave you (Ephesians 4:32)

At Christmastime we like to show our love for our families and friends by giving them cards and gifts. We can also show our love for those in our family by being kind and helpful to them.

From now until Christmas we could play a game that would help us show our love for someone in our family.

Let's write our name on a slip of paper, fold it over, and mix up the slips. Each one takes a slip. Don't let anyone see the name you have. Let's keep it a secret until Christmas Eve. From now until Christmas we'll try to do secret, happy things for the person whose name we choose.

Since we won't know who chose our name, we won't know who is doing secret, kind things for us. We might be surprised to find ourselves feeling thankful to everyone in the family because of the kind, thoughtful things one person is doing for us.

Let's join hands and pray that God will help us be kind, patient, and forgiving to those in our family.

PRAY: Dear Lord, here we are joined in a circle of love. We want to show our love for each other every day. Amen.

SING: *Third stanza of "O little town of Bethlehem,"* printed on page 40.

(The candle of promise and the candle of light may be lit.)

READ *(as someone lights the third candle):* We call the third candle of Advent, *love.* Love makes us want to help others.

Let us consider how to stir up one another to love and good works (Hebrews 10:24).

Stevie dropped his books on the kitchen table and slid into the chair.

"You're late from school," his mother said. "You want some milk and cookies?"

"I'm not hungry," Stevie said.

"Are you sick?" his mother asked.

"Nope." Stevie took a big breath. "Dave's the new boy in school. His father left home last week, and his mother says there won't be money for Christmas presents. Dave doesn't care, but he has a little brother and sister. They won't understand about no Christmas presents."

Jesus told his followers they were to love and help anyone who is in trouble. What can our family do this Advent season to show love for those who need help?
(Members of the family may make suggestions.)

Would you like to know what Stevie did? He took some of his allowance and bought little presents for Dave's brother and sister. Stevie's mother baked a special Christmas bread and a box of cookies, and Stevie took them to Dave's house.

PRAY: Dear Lord, thank you for the good things you give us. Help us to be willing to show our love to those who need help.

SING: *First stanza of "O little town of Bethlehem,"
printed on page 39.*

READ *(as someone lights the candles):* We light the candle of love to remind us God wants us to love everyone, even people we call our enemies.

"But I say to you, Love your enemies" (Matthew 5:44).

Sometimes when we get very angry with someone, we say, "I hate him. He's my enemy." Fortunately, after a while we usually forgive the person who made us angry, and then we are friends again.

When people stay enemies for a long time terrible things can happen. They sometimes try to kill each other, and they even start wars.

During World War 2 an American pilot was getting ready to bomb a building in Japan. He took aim, and the bomb fell, but for some reason it did not explode.

After the war the pilot became a salesman. Over the years he did a lot of traveling and made many friends. One of his friends was a Japanese businessman.

The salesman was happy he could be friends with the man from Japan. The war had been over for many years, and he was glad he didn't have to think of the Japanese people as enemies any longer.

The Japanese businessman showed the salesman some pictures of Japan. One picture showed the building where the businessman had worked during the war. The salesman stared at the picture. Suddenly he realized this was the building he almost bombed when he was a pilot.

PRAY: Dear God, when we become angry with other people, help us to forgive them. Please show us how to love others, even those who seem to be our enemies.

SING: *Second stanza of "O little town of Bethlehem," printed on page 40.*

READ (*as someone lights the candles*): Promise—God keeps his promise. Light—Jesus said, "I am the Light of the world." Love—God loves us. We must remember to love and encourage other Christians.

Therefore encourage one another and build one another up, just as you are doing (1 Thessalonians 5:11).

St. Paul wrote letters to the people in the early churches. He wanted the congregations to know he was thinking about them and praying for them. He wanted to remind them of God's love for them.

When we receive letters and cards during the Christmas season we are happy to know our friends have remembered us. If we are worried about something, a note or word of encouragement can give us strength.

God wants us to love everyone, but it is especially important for us to care about our fellow Christians. When Christians become discouraged, words of love and concern from fellow believers can help build up faith.

When we talk about "fellow Christians" we mean not only the people in our own church congregation, but also Christians everywhere. Perhaps someone in our family knows of a fellow Christian who needs encouragement right now. (*Family members may suggest names.*) We could include a note or letter with our Christmas card to remind them of God's love and our concern for them.

PRAY: Dear Lord, thank you for all the people who love us and encourage us. Help us show love and concern for others. Amen.

SING: *Third stanza of "O little town of Bethlehem," printed on page 40.*

READ *(as someone lights the candles):* The candle of love
reminds us that God wants us to share the good news of his
love with people all over the world.

Sing to the Lord, bless his name;
**   tell of his salvation from day to day.**
Declare his glory among the nations,
**   his marvelous works among all the peoples** (Psalm 96:2-3).

God wants people all over the world to know how much he
loves them. A Sunday school song reminds us of this love.

Jesus loves the little children,
All the children of the world.
Red and yellow, black and white,
All are precious in his sight.
Jesus loves the little children of the world.

In one church a special Advent wreath is used as a reminder
of God's love for the world's people. The wreath is so large
none of us could get our arms around it.

You might be surprised at the colors of the candles. One is
red, another yellow, a third black, and the fourth white. The
candles represent the people of the many different nations of
the world. On each Sunday of Advent, as a different color
candle is lit, people in the church pray especially for the nations which the candle represents. The people in the church
often collect money to help people all over the world. They
know that by helping others they can share the good news
of God's love for everyone.

PRAY: Dear God, people all over the world need to know
how much you love them. Help us to share the good news
of your love. Amen.

SING: *Second stanza of "O little town of Bethlehem,"*
printed on page 40.

READ (as someone lights the candles): God's promise to send a Savior took a long time. As the candle of light flames, we remember that Jesus said, "I am the Light of the world." We light the candle of love. God first loved us, so we love him and others. The fourth candle is called *hope*. The candle of hope reminds us that God gave us a gift of hope— life forever with him.

"And when I go to prepare a place for you, I will come again and will take you to myself, that where I am you may be also" (John 14:3).

An eight-year-old Korean orphan learned he was to fly across the ocean to be adopted by American parents who had prepared a home for him. Thinking about the big change in his life gave him a pain in his stomach. He didn't know the family or where he would be living. He wasn't sure if there was such a place. Still he hoped he would like his new home and that his new parents would love him.

At the airport they welcomed him with bright new clothes and presents. Everything about America was different. The language, the food, his own room, school, church. But his new parents showed their love for him and taught him about God, so that he soon learned to love them.

After a year or two it was time for adoption proceedings. Together they answered questions and the adoption papers were signed.

A few days later the boy said, "That was when I knew you really loved me. I always hoped you did and that I could stay. But then I knew."

"What do you mean?" his parents asked.

"The day you adopted me I knew you really loved me."

The Bible tells us that if we have opened our heart's door

to Jesus, we have been adopted into the family of God. When Jesus went back to heaven, he said that he would prepare a place for us, and some day he would come for us so we could live with him. Knowing that Jesus has made a special place for us in heaven gives us hope.

PRAY: Dear Father in heaven, we worship the baby Jesus, born in a stable, and we rejoice that he loved us and became our Savior. Now we are hoping for what we have never seen— life forever with Jesus, our king. Amen.

SING: *First stanza of "Beautiful Savior," printed on page 40.*

READ *(as someone lights the candles):* The fourth candle of Advent reminds us of the hope the Holy Spirit gives us. Jesus knew his followers would be lonely without him, so he told them about a plan he had, something they could hope for.

"I will pray the Father, and he will give you another Counselor [the Holy Spirit], to be with you for ever" (John 14:16).

A woman whose husband had died moved into an apartment. To help her, a nephew hauled several loads of heavy boxes in his station wagon. Afterwards, she invited her nephew and niece and five children for dinner.

The seven-year-old asked, "Do you have to live all alone in this apartment?"

"Yes," she said.

The girl, thinking of the love and closeness in her family, said, "I'm sorry you have to live alone."

With a smile the woman answered, "I'm not really alone, for I have God's Holy Spirit to comfort me."

Jesus' disciples felt sad when he said he was going away, until Jesus told them about the Holy Spirit. That gave them hope. When the Holy Spirit came they were joyful.

We have that hope too—that the Holy Spirit will be with us. He will be our helper and teach us all things. That's something to hope for!

PRAY: Spirit of God, teach us to feel that you are always near. Fill us with the special hope only you can give. Amen.

SING: *Second stanza of "Beautiful Savior," printed on page 40.*

(The candle of promise, the candle of light, and the candle of love may be lit.)

READ *(as someone lights the fourth candle):* The candle of hope reminds us of what the Bible calls our "blessed hope."
We have this hope because we know Jesus will come again.

. . . awaiting our blessed hope, the appearing of the glory of our great God and Savior Jesus Christ (Titus 2:13).

Jesus was ready to return to his throne in heaven, so he called his apostles around him, Peter and James and John and the others. He wanted to give them a few last instructions.

The disciples asked him questions. "Lord," they said, "surely now you will set up your great kingdom on earth."

But that wasn't what Jesus had in mind at all. Gently he told them only God the Father knew when Jesus would return to earth and set up his kingdom.

And right before their eyes Jesus was lifted up and disappeared in a cloud. Can't you see how their mouths fell open and their eyes got big as they stared at the cloud? Then two men dressed in white stood beside them.

"No use looking at the sky," they said. "Just as Jesus went away he will come again."

Knowing that Jesus would come again filled the disciples with hope and joy.

PRAY: Dear God, thank you for the wonderful hope that is ours because we know Jesus will come again. Amen.

SING: *Second stanza of "Beautiful Savior," printed on page 40.*

READ *(as someone lights the candles):* We light four candles on the Advent wreath. For almost four weeks we have been getting ready for the celebration of Christ's coming at Christmas. When we hope for some big event, like a birthday or vacation, we don't forget all about it. We try to be ready. The candle of hope reminds us we must be ready.

"You also must be ready; for the Son of man is coming at an unexpected hour" (Luke 12:40).

When it was time for Jesus to return to his Father in heaven, the disciples were told that he would come to earth again. At first the disciples expected Jesus to come back right away. They probably didn't think long years would go by. Then they remembered that Jesus had told them they were to be witnesses for him.

A witness tells what he has seen, what has happened to him. The disciples loved Jesus and wanted everybody to know about his life and death. We too can talk about Jesus and be witnesses for him.

The way to be ready for Jesus is to love him, tell others about him, obey him, and love one another.

PRAY: O Lord, we want to be ready. Fill us with hope as we wait for your coming. Amen.

SING: *Third stanza of "Beautiful Savior," printed on page 40.*

READ *(as someone lights the candles):* The fourth candle of
Advent reminds us that the Holy Spirit can fill us with hope.

By the power of the Holy Spirit you may abound in hope
(Romans 15:13b).

Franz Gruber sat down to practice for the Christmas Eve
service at the church in Oberndorf, Austria, in 1818, but no
sound came from the organ. He was ready to give up.
He could see there was no hope for the old organ. Just then
the young priest of the church, Josef Mohr, climbed the steps
to the organ loft.

"It is badly in need of repair, isn't it?" he asked.

"What a disaster," the organist said. "There's no time to get
it repaired before the Christmas Eve service."

"Here," the pastor said, holding out a slip of paper. "I wrote
the words for a song, a lullaby. I hope you can write the
music. You can play your guitar while we sing."

"A guitar in church? On Christmas Eve, when they are
expecting organ music?" Franz Gruber shook his head, but he
read the words quickly, "Silent night, holy night." The simple
lines about the birth of Christ excited him. How he hoped
he could compose fitting music!

When the church bells called the people to the Christmas
Eve service, no organ music greeted them. Instead the pastor
and the organist, accompanied by the guitar, sang the tender
words of "Silent night, holy night."

Today no Christmas celebration is complete without the
song, because it reminds us of the gift of hope God gave us
that "Silent night."

SING: *"Silent night, holy night."*

PRAY: Dear God, may your Holy Spirit fill us with hope to
overcome problems in our everyday life. Amen.

READ *(as someone lights the candles):* All Christians share God's promises and the light, love, and hope Jesus brought into the world when he was born. The candle of hope reminds us that God's gift of hope is with us even when we are far away from home.

May the God of hope fill you with all joy and peace (Romans 15:13a).

It was Christmas Eve in Frankfort, Germany, with snow falling like white feathers. A young man in town on business over the Christmas season felt lonely. It wasn't much fun being so far from his family and friends. All around him people hurried about their own business. Even if he stopped someone to talk, it wouldn't help. He couldn't speak or understand German.

Down the street he heard church bells ring. He decided to go inside for the Christmas Eve service.

In the German church people stood in rows, since there were no benches or pews. The minister wore a wide pleated collar that stuck out like a box, called a ruff, and a square shaped hat sat on his head. He spoke in German, and, of course, the young man couldn't understand him.

Then the organ burst into music he did understand. All around him people sang "Stille Nacht, heilige Nacht." The man let his voice ring out too. "Silent night, holy night." The words were different, but the music was the same.

The hope God gives can go with us wherever we are.

PRAY: O Lord, we praise you that wherever we go there are those who love you to give us hope and encouragement. Amen.

SING: *Third stanza of "Beautiful Savior," printed on page 40.*

READ *(as someone lights the candles):* This is the last time this year we will light the Advent candles. For four weeks the candles have been burning as we thought about God's promises to us, about the light his coming brings to us, about his love for us, and about our hope in him. We have been thinking of God's gift to us—Jesus, our Savior. During this Advent season we have been getting our hearts ready for Christmas.

Listen to the story of Jesus' birth. (Read Luke 2:1-20.)

Let's hold hands around the table. Each one of us may say a short prayer of thanks for what we have learned this Advent.

PRAY *(after individual prayers have been said):* Dear God, thank you for the special times we have spent together this Advent as we learned more about your gift to us—Jesus, our Savior. Amen.

SING: O come, all ye faithful, joyful and triumphant,
        O come ye, O come ye to Bethlehem;
        Come and behold him born the King of angels:
        O come, let us adore him, O come, let us adore him,
        O come, let us adore him, Christ the Lord!

(Members of the family may reveal the names they chose, the person they have secretly shown kindness to during Advent.)

(Although different hymn stanzas could be sung each day, the family may prefer to repeat the first stanza of a hymn throughout the week.)

1 **O come, O come, Emmanuel,**
   And ransom captive Israel,
   That mourns in lonely exile here
   Until the Son of God appear.
   Rejoice, rejoice! Emmanuel
   Shall come to thee, O Israel.

2 O come, O come, thou Lord of Might,
   Who to thy tribes, on Sinai's height,
   In ancient times didst give the law
   In cloud, and majesty, and awe.
   Rejoice, rejoice! Emmanuel
   Shall come to thee, O Israel.

3 O come, thou Rod of Jesse, free
   Thine own from Satan's tyranny;
   From depths of hell thy people save,
   And give them victory o'er the grave.
   Rejoice, rejoice! Emmanuel
   Shall come to thee, O Israel.

4 O come, thou Dayspring, come and cheer
   Our spirits by thine advent here;
   Disperse the gloomy clouds of night,
   And death's dark shadows put to flight.
   Rejoice, rejoice! Emmanuel
   Shall come to thee, O Israel.

1 **Thou didst leave thy throne**
And thy kingly crown
When thou camest to earth for me,
But in Bethlehem's home
Was there found no room
For thy holy nativity:
O come to my heart, Lord Jesus;
There is room in my heart for thee.

2 Heaven's arches rang
When the angels sang,
Proclaiming thy royal degree;
But in lowly birth
Didst thou come to earth,
And in great humility:
O come to my heart, Lord Jesus;
There is room in my heart for thee.

3 Thou camest, O Lord,
With the living word,
That should set thy people free;
But with mocking scorn,
And with crown of thorn,
They bore thee to Calvary:
O come to my heart, Lord Jesus;
There is room in my heart for thee.

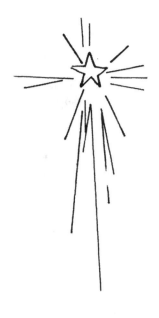

1 **O little town of Bethlehem,**
How still we see thee lie!
Above thy deep and dreamless sleep
The silent stars go by;
Yet in thy dark streets shineth
The everlasting Light;
The hopes and fears of all the years
Are met in thee tonight.

2   For Christ is born of Mary,
    And gathered all above,
    While mortals sleep, the angels keep
    Their watch of wondering love.
    O morning stars, together
    Proclaim the holy birth,
    And praises sing to God the King,
    And peace to men on earth!

3   O holy Child of Bethlehem,
    Descend to us, we pray;
    Cast out our sin, and enter in,
    Be born in us today.
    We hear the Christmas angels
    The great glad tidings tell;
    O come to us, abide with us,
    Our Lord Immanuel!

1   **Beautiful Savior,**
    King of Creation,
    Son of God and Son of Man!
    Truly I'd love thee,
    Truly I'd serve thee,
    Light of my soul, my joy, my crown.

2   Fair are the meadows,
    Fair are the woodlands,
    Robed in flowers of blooming spring;
    Jesus is fairer,
    Jesus is purer,
    He makes our sorrowing spirit sing.

3   Beautiful Savior,
    Lord of the nations,
    Son of God and Son of Man!
    Glory and honor,
    Praise, adoration,
    Now and for evermore be thine!